JEFF TOGHILL

Sailboarding for Beginners

W·W·NORTON & COMPANY
New York · London

Copyright © 1984 by Jeff Toghill
All rights reserved.
Published simultaneously in Canada by Penguin Books Canada Ltd., 2801 John Street, Markham, Ontario L3R 1B4.
Printed in the United States of America.

Library of Congress Cataloging-in-Publication Data
Toghill, Jeff E.
  Sailboarding for beginners.
  Originally published: South Melbourne, Victoria, Australia : Sun Books, 1984.
  1. Windsurfing. I. Title.
GV811.63.W56T64 1986   797.3'3   85–18835

ISBN 0-393-30299-7

W. W. Norton & Company, Inc., 500 Fifth Avenue, New York, N.Y. 10110
W. W. Norton & Company Ltd., 37 Great Russell Street, London WC1B 3NU

1 2 3 4 5 6 7 8 9 0

Contents

Introduction 4
The board 6
The rig 8
Types of boards 10
Sails 12
The right clothes 13
How a sailboard works 14
Getting started 16
Rigging the board 18
Launching 20
Balance 22
Turning the board 23
Starting to sail 24
Steering the board 26
Port tack and starboard tack 27
The sailing positions 28
Manoeuvring the board 29
The non-sailing zone 30
Tacking 31

Gybing 33
Sailing round the compass 34
Tacking to windward 36
The sailing rules 37
Safety 38
Emergency 40
Hypothermia 42
Strong wind sailing 44
Racing 48
Using a harness 50
Footwook 51
Freestyle 52
Wave riding 54
Hints on wave riding 55
Surfing 56
Etiquette 58
Four sailboarding knots 60
Some popular sailboarding terms 62

Introduction

There can be few outdoor sports that have caught the imagination as much as sailboarding. From humble beginnings in the late 1960s and early 1970s, grew a new concept in sailing that spread like a bushfire across the water sports scene. Although originating in California, sailboarding gained its initial impetus in Europe where, between 1973 and 1978, an estimated 150,000 sailboards were sold. But this was just the beginning. As enthusiasm for the sport grew, boundaries diminished and by the 1980s the exhilarating little craft had spread its colourful sails across the entire world.

Countries orientated to water sports such as the U.S.A., Australia and South Africa hailed sailboarding as the greatest thing since the invention of the surf board. Surprisingly, the same enthusiasm came from countries such as Scandinavia and Canada where seasonal limits should have curtailed interest in the sport. But so exhilarating and exciting was this new aspect of sailing that it transcended all boundaries of race, creed and climate.

The challenge of the sailboard is akin to that of the hang glider. It is a total gauntlet throwdown to the elements. It is individual man against individual nature—a personal, intimate challenge. A challenge in which the will to win becomes more stimulated with every setback. It is an adrenalin catalyst. A sport of addiction. A personal Everest.

Yet it is also a sport for all ages. A sport for all philosophies. It is cheap enough for youngsters to enjoy, yet rewarding enough to kindle enthusiasm in those who have done it all. It transcends the pace of modern living and provides a perfect panacea for work-jaded bodies. It is, without question, the sport of the 20th century.

The board

The standard sailboard is made from fibreglass or polyethylene with a polyurethane foam core. It is therefore virtually maintenance free and under normal circumstances is indestructable. It is not affected by heat or cold or most chemicals it is likely to encounter, and is unsinkable, even when the outer casing is punctured. Most standard boards are around 3.5 metres (11 ft 6 in) long by around 0.7 metres (2 ft 3 in) wide and weigh in around 18 kg (40 lb).

The board has a recess for the **mast step** and a slot for the **dagger board**. It may be raised at the bow, as is usually the case with wave-riding boards, and is fitted with a **skeg** under the stern to give directional stability. This is a flexible fin which may be permanently attached or screwed in place for sailing. Skegs vary in shape according to the designer's ideas. Compare the difference between Windsurfer and Windglider skegs—the former is short and pointed, the latter long and flat.

The dagger board may also be of different shapes, but the standard shape follows the centreboard of a sailing boat in a roughly rectangular form angled towards the stern. The dagger board is totally retractable since it is not required when the board is sailing downwind. When on or across the wind, the dagger board prevents the sailboard from slipping sideways across the water, giving it a good 'bite' to drive it forward. It is usually made from fibreglass, although some are made from timber, and is fitted with a strap to enable it to be retracted.

As will be seen later, sailboards come in many different shapes and sizes and may be fitted with extra equipment such as toe straps.

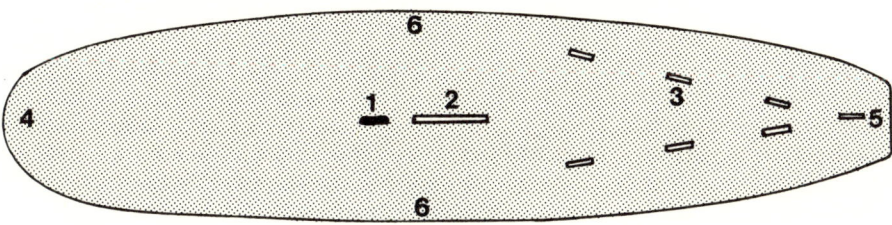

1. Mast step
2. Dagger board
3. Foot straps
4. The bow
5. The stern
6. Rails
7. Skeg

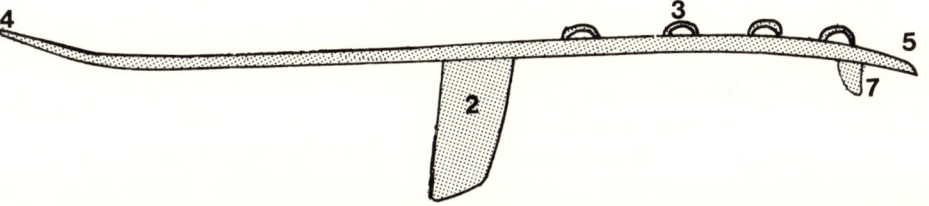

The rig

The **mast** of a sailboard is usually made from extruded aluminium tube or fibreglass and is very flexible, being tapered towards the top to increase flexibility. It is around 4.2 metres (13 ft 9 in) long and is mounted on a universal joint which enables it to be moved in any direction. It fits inside a sleeve on the sail and usually has some form of plug or sealing device at the top to prevent the mast filling with water.

The **mast foot** fits into or around the bottom of the mast and is connected to a **universal joint** which in turn is mounted on a mast step fitting or plug. This plug drops into a recess on the board through which the drive in the sail is transmitted to the board. Also near the mast foot is a fitting for the **downhaul**, the rope which stretches the leading edge of the sail.

The **wishbone boom** is secured to the mast by a rope called the **inhaul** which gives it good freedom of movement. The boom passes down either side of the sail and is secured to the clew of the sail by another rope, known as the **outhaul**. Yet another rope is attached to the front of the boom, usually adjacent to its **handle**, and this is called an **uphaul** since it is used for pulling the rig up out of the water.

The sail is made from synthetic cloth around 5.574 sq metres (60 sq ft) in area on a standard rig. The **luff** of the sail is the front or leading edge, the **leech** the back or trailing edge, and the **foot** is the bottom of the sail. **Battens** are inserted into the leech to provide rigidity while the luff is in the form of a sleeve, allowing the mast to be threaded into the sail. There are numerous different sizes and shapes of sails, some of which are designed for strong winds, and some for special work, such as racing or wave jumping. A plastic window is fitted into the sail to allow visibility when sailing on the downwind or 'lee' side.

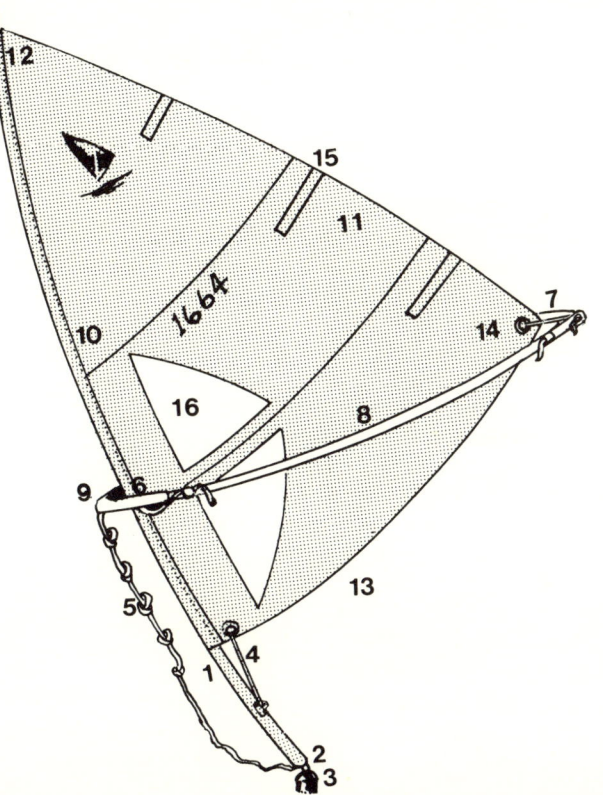

1. Mast
2. Mast foot
3. Universal joint
4. Downhaul
5. Uphaul
6. Inhaul
7. Outhaul
8. Boom
9. Handle
10. Luff
11. Leech
12. Peak
13. Foot
14. Clew
15. Battens
16. Window

Types of boards

The main differences between sailboards relates to the type of sailing they will be used for. There are boards for training beginners, which are obviously very stable and with relatively small sails. There are boards for racing with every refinement that can be fitted. And there are boards for wave jumping.

The **Windsurfer** and the **Windglider** are both recognised international class boards within the IYRU (International Yacht Racing Union) and are therefore to be found anywhere in the world. Other boards such as the **Mistral** and **Dufour** are also marketed across the world, and there are many locally-designed boards constructed specifically for local conditions.

Learning boards
Designed with extra width and buoyancy to give them greater stability and usually with a smaller rig, these are ideal boards on which to begin sailboarding.

Fun boards
These are the standard sailboards with reasonable stability, quick response, moderate price and a wide variety of uses.

Racing boards
Racing boards, like all racing craft, sacrifice some qualities in order to go fast. They are rounded off more on the underside and the bow is shaped to form a V section for better upwind performance. They usually have greater displacement but are less stable than standard boards.

Wave jumping boards
Wave boards are generally shorter than standard boards and are fitted with footstraps so that the board can be controlled, even when it is in the air.

Sails

There is a sail to suit every every type of board, every wind condition and every skill level. The standard sized sail which is used in normal conditions is somewhere between 4.65 sq m (50 sq ft) and 5.6 sq m (60 sq ft) in area, its precise size being determined by the type of board. Smaller sails are used for strong wind conditions or sail training, while big, light sails are used for light weather. Sails are made of synthetic cloth and have a large window to give good visibility when sailing.

Maxi-rigs
Usually used in open class sailing, maxi-sails are designed for very light weather and can have a surface area as large as 8.4 sq m (90 sq ft). A special mast extension is necessary for sails of this type.

Regatta sails
These sails are often made of slightly thicker sailcloth than usual to allow better shape retention. 'One-design' racing sails are cut to computer specifications as they are with conventional sailboats, thus ensuring that no one sail has any advantage over another.

Wave sails
The cut of a wave-riding sail differs from the standard by virtue of its higher-cut clew. This prevents the sail from dragging in the water when sheeting on after a jump or when accelerating on a wave.

Kid's rig
Obviously a smaller sail to match the lesser weight of young sailors, the surface area of this sail is usually less than 3.7 sq m (40 sq ft). To match the sail, a smaller rig is required with a shorter mast and boom. Smaller boards may also be used, but as a rule the kid's rig will fit a standard sized board so that the same board

can be used with different rigs and thus provide enjoyment for the whole family.

The right clothes

One of the few dangers in sailboarding comes from the complete exposure to the elements. Unlike any other type of sailing, you are frequently dunked in the water and then exposed, fully standing, to the wind. Even in warm climates this can cause problems. While it may be hot on the beach when you launch the board, it will certainly be much cooler as you get out into the wind and even colder after your first dunking. Protection from the cold is one of the prime factors of safety in sailboarding.

Hypothermia is insidious. It lowers the 'deep' body temperature to the point where vital organs are affected and may cease to operate. Constant immersion can cause hypothermia even in relatively warm water, and immersion and exposure to cool winds can bring it on even faster. Jumpers and T-shirts can be worn in warm weather, but the only real protection comes from wetsuits. They come in a variety of thicknesses for different conditions.

A different problem arises with exposure to the sun. Excessive exposure can cause extremely painful sunburn and even lead to melanoma—an often terminal form of skin cancer. Sun creams, peaked caps and clothing, although seemingly unsuited to sailboarding, are advisable if you are sailing for lengthy periods on sunny days.

How a sailboard works

On the beach, a sailboard appears very simple but it is actually the result of a very complex design. The principle difference between a sailboard and a sailboat is that since the sailboard has no rudder, it must steer by its sails.

The curve in the sail, known as an aerofoil section, makes the wind flow faster round the outside than the inside of the curve and this creates a vortex or suction behind the sail which pulls the board along. Most of this suction is sideways, so the board will skitter sideways across the water unless some other factor is introduced to correct it.

By lowering the dagger board, a flat surface is presented to the water to resist any sideways movement but allow forward movement. Now we have two forces, one acting through the sail and attempting to push the board sideways, and another in the water pushing in the opposite direction on the dagger board. Just as an orange pip squeezed between finger and thumb will fly forwards, the board, literally squeezed between wind pressure and water resistance, will also fly forward.

Centres of Effort and Lateral Resistance

The theoretical point on the sails through which the wind forces act is called the **Centre of Effort** (CE). The point on the dagger board where the resisting forces of the water act is called the **Centre of Lateral Resistance** (CLR). If these two centres are located diametrically opposite one another, then the board will move directly forward. If the CE is located ahead of the CLR, the pressure of wind in the sail will push the bow away and the board will sheer away from the wind. The reverse applies if the CE is behind the CLR.

The CLR cannot be moved, since the dagger board is a permanent fixture, but the sail can be moved forward and backward, and therefore the CE can be moved in front of or behind the CLR. This is how a sailboard is steered. By tilting the sail forward, the bow is made to bear away from the wind and by tilting it back, the board is made to swing up into the wind.

Illustrating how the dagger board sticks down beneath the sailboard to create lateral resistance, countering the sideways push of the sail.

Getting started

Before you get the board in the water there are a few basics which not only make life easy, but indicate that you know what you are about. Nothing brands you as a rookie more than having the board the wrong way on the car or being all fists and thumbs carrying it down the beach. And when the sail takes off along the beach with you in tow like a drunken hang glider, you have really established yourself as belonging to the lunatic fringe! Make sure the board is always secured firmly on the roof rack of your car with the bow forward and the mast and boom alongside. It will be embarrassing and costly if you accelerate away from traffic lights leaving your board and rig sticking ignominiously out of the windscreen of the car behind.

And you will not be popular with the beach crowd if, when launching, you poke your mast into sunbathers, drop the board on someone's toe or try to smother them with five-and-a-half square metres of sailcloth.

It is known in some sports as etiquette, in others as plain commonsense. Either way it makes life easier and less traumatic when you are a beginner.

- Tie the board and rig securely onto the car. Shock cord or expanding luggage straps are often suitable.
- Carry the board by means of the dagger board or mast slot, with the top of the board closest to the body.
- When carrying the rig, hold it over your head with the mast horizontal and the boom aligned with the wind direction.
- If it is too windy or dangerous to carry the rig, adopt the same position but drag it along the beach.

Rigging the board

Assuming that you have assembled the basic equipment, the following procedure is adopted when rigging most sailboards.
1. Insert the mast into the sleeve of the sail and secure it with the downhaul. Apply moderate tension to the downhaul in normal conditions. Apply increased tension for stronger winds.

2. Slip the boom over the sail to its correct position, then tilt it to align with the mast.

3. Secure the inhaul to the mast at the sleeve hole by means of a Prusik knot, a rolling hitch or a double clove hitch (see Pages 60–61), and attach the boom. Secure the end of the inhaul in a cleat.

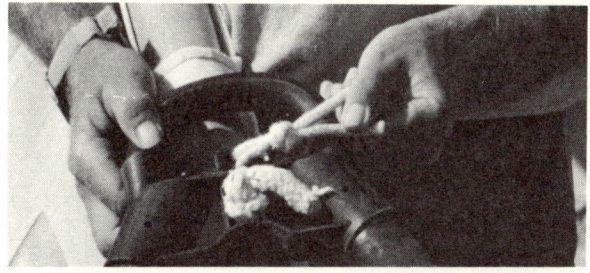

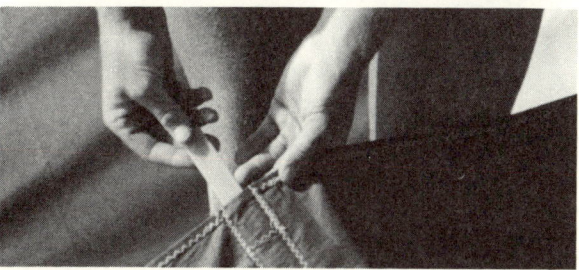

4. Fit the battens firmly into the leech of the sail.
5. Bring the outer end of the boom down to its normal position and secure the clew of the sail to the outer end of the boom with the outhaul. Tension this line according to wind strengths, as with the downhaul.
6. Secure the uphaul to the boom or handle. Plug the mast foot into the mast step and the dagger board into its slot.

Launching

For your first few sails, a quiet spot with wind across or onto the beach is preferable. Nothing is more frightening than finding yourself getting farther and farther out and not knowing how to get back. This can happen with an offshore wind, so chose any wind except one blowing off the beach.

Similarly, even the smallest waves will give you trouble as you try to get your balance. The surf can come later so pick a beach with no waves for your early training attempts.

A beach without too many swimmers is also a plus, since you will not be popular if you crown a few heads with your mast, and for the first few days your rig will probably be in the water more than out of it.

Buddy sailing with a friend will give you confidence and make fun out of frustration. You can also learn a lot from watching others make mistakes!

1. Find a quiet spot to begin your training, well away from people and hazards.

2. Throw the rig into the water and connect up with the board well clear of the beach and swimmers.
3. If there is no suitable spot at the beach, paddle out until you find one.

4. Launching through surf takes a lot of skill.

Balance

This is the part beginners find hardest. Being able to stand on the board seems an almost unattainable goal, let alone doing anything with sails! Yet, like all new things, it comes with practice. A good way to begin is to get the feel of the static board. Take the board into shallow water and physically turn it until it is across wind. Holding the uphaul as a means of support, stand upright on the board with your back to the wind. When you get the feel of this, start moving around the board, still using the uphaul as a support (it is mostly psychological, but it works!)

When you have become familiar with the trembling board beneath your feet, get into the starting position. This is as before, with the board

across the wind and your back to the wind with your feet placed one on either side of the mast on the centreline of the board. Now lean back, bend your knees and start to pull up the mast. Straighten your knees as the mast comes upright, keeping your back straight and not leaning forward. With the mast upright, hold onto it and let it flap in the wind, once again getting used to the feel of things.

Turning the board

Having got the feel of the static board, now start to manoeuvre it beneath your feet. Turning the board relies to a certain extent on inclining the mast, but footwork is also important, and you can learn this while getting your balance.

Hold the boom by the handle (or uphaul) with the sail still flapping idly, and transfer your weight to your back foot. Immediately you will feel a response from the board which will begin to turn into the wind. As it turns, walk slowly around the mast, using your other hand if required, until you are on the opposite side of the board. Continue your walk, turning the board through a full circle to get back to your starting position.

Now try it the other way round, and continue to practice until you feel confident and lose some of that initial wobbliness!

Starting to sail

By now you should have your balance and be able to turn the static board with your feet. It is time to start sailing. Get into the starting position again, for all attempts must start from this position. If you fall off, you must always revert to the starting position before attempting to get the board going again. Briefly repeated, the starting position is:
1. Feet on the centreline of the board.
2. One before the mast, one on the dagger board.
3. Back to the wind.
4. Board across the wind.

Pull up the mast as described earlier. Hold it by the handle or uphaul while you get yourself together. Relax. Then start sailing:
- Lean back to bring the mast upright on the centreline of the board.
- Hold the handle or uphaul with your back hand (nearest the stern) and cross your forward hand over it to grasp the boom about 15 cm (6 in) back.
- Hold the mast in position with this hand and relocate your back hand a comfortable distance down the boom.
- Lean back and pull in the boom with the back hand, at the same time tilting the mast forward with the front hand. The board will start to move forward. At any time you feel unbalanced, let go the back hand and start again.

Steering the board

- To steer the board into the wind, tilt the mast back.

- To steer the board away from the wind, tilt the mast forward.

Port tack and starboard tack

- A board is on a port tack when the wind comes over the left side.

- A board is on a starboard tack when the wind is on the right side.

The sailing positions

A board is said to be **close-hauled** when she is sailing close to the wind. The sail is hauled in close and the dagger board is right down.

With the wind on the beam (about 90 degrees from the bow) the board is **reaching**. The sail is eased out to an angle of about 45 degrees to the centreline of the board.

With the wind behind, the board is **running free**. The sail is eased out until it is at right angles to the centreline of the board and the dagger board is taken out.

Manoeuvring the board

From the previous pages it can be seen that full control of the board is gained by combining the various actions of tilting the mast and pulling in or letting out the sail (called **sheeting**). The board can be sailed up towards the wind or turned away from it and it can be speeded up or slowed down. Assuming the board is in the basic starting position, the various manoeuvres can be carried out as follows:
1. Sheet on, mast forward, the board will begin to move and bear away from the wind.
2. Ease the sail out further, mast forward, the board will bear away to the reaching position.
3. Ease sail right out, mast still forward, the board will swing away to the running position.
4. Sheet in the sail, mast back, the board will round up to the reaching position.
5. Sheet in tight, mast back, she will fly up to the close-hauled position.

The non-sailing zone

The closest an average sailboard can sail to the wind is at an angle of about 45 degrees to the wind. If she sails any closer, the wind will get round the luff and collapse the sail, causing the board to stall. This means that no sailboard can sail within a 90 degree zone (45 degrees on either side of the wind) under any circumstances. This is known as the **non-sailing zone**, and a board sailing in the close-hauled position is sailing as close to the wind as possible and therefore on the edge of that non-sailing zone.

In effect, this means that a sailboard can sail in any direction around the compass outside the non-sailing zone, simply by adjusting her sails and tilting her mast. But she cannot sail closer to the wind than about 45 degrees.

Tacking

It is impossible for a board to sail directly into the wind or even at an angle of less than 45 degrees on either side of the wind because of the non-sailing zone. And yet, to be fully manoeuvrable the board must be able to make progress to windward. While there is no way she can be made to sail inside the non-sailing zone, she can be made to sail across it from one tack to another. This is known as **tacking**.

Since the board will lose speed and begin to stall when she enters the non-sailing zone, her approach must ensure that she has the shortest distance to travel across the zone and has sufficient speed to carry her through to the other side. Two factors must be checked in order to do this: The board must be moving fast. It must be in the close-hauled position.

When these conditions exist, then tacking is carried out as described below.

- Tilt the mast well back and release your back hand from the boom as she rounds up to the wind. Start to walk round the front of the mast.
- Walk right round the mast, turning the board with your feet and changing hands on the handle or uphaul.
- When the board is across the wind, lean the mast forward, sheet in the sail and start sailing on the other tack.

Gybing

Changing tack with the wind astern is much easier, because there is no non-sailing zone to pass through. It is called **gybing**.
- Ease away to the running free position with the sail right across the board.
- Release the boom from the sheeting hand. It will swing forward, and across the bow. Change hands on the handle or uphaul.
- Take up the boom again with the opposite hand and sheet on as required. The board will have gybed from one tack to the other.

Sailing round the compass

Now the board has been sailed through all possible sailing positions, and it remains only to combine them to achieve total control. The best way to put this into practice is to sail right around the compass. Assuming we start in the close-hauled position on a port tack, the procedure will be:
1. Mast forward, ease sail out, bear away to a reach.
2. Mast forward, ease sail out all the way, bear away to a run.
3. Gybe the sail, board now running free on a starboard tack.
4. Mast back, sheet in the sail, close up to a reach.
5. Mast back, sheet in all the way, board is now close-hauled on a starboard tack.
6. Mast back, change sides, board tacks across to the close-hauled position on a port tack. She has now sailed right around the compass.

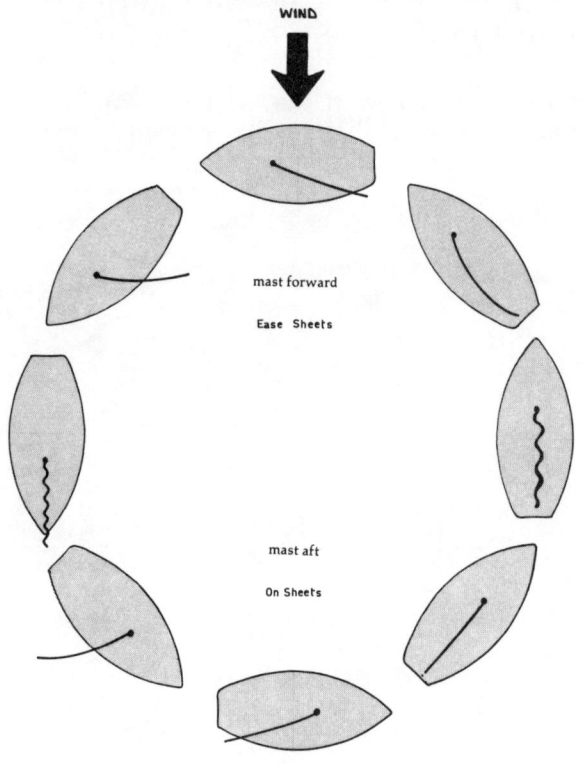

35

Tacking to windward

We have already seen that under no circumstances can a board sail closer to the wind than around 45 degrees. So what happens when your destination is directly to windward?

The answer is that instead of sailing directly towards your destination (which is impossible anyway), you zigzag into the wind sailing first on one tack then the other. By sailing up as close to the wind as possible on the first tack, you will be aiming to within 45 degrees of your objective, but not directly at it.

When a board tacks it passes through an angle of around 90 degrees. So if you sail on the first tack until the objective is 90 degrees (on the beam), then when you tack you will be pointing directly at it. In practice, shorter tacks are usually made so that the board progresses towards her destination in a series of zigzags. This is known as **beating** or **tacking to windward** and is the only way a sailcraft of any type can make progress into the wind.

The sailing rules

The sailing rules apply to all sailcraft, including sailboards, and are international, so they apply to waterways all over the world. The principal rules are:
1. Sailcraft sailing on a port tack give way to sailcraft sailing on a starboard tack.
2. When both are sailing on the same tack, the sailcraft which gets the wind first (the windward craft) gives way to the other.
3. Any craft overtaking another must keep clear of the overtaken craft.
4. Power craft give way to sailcraft except when being overtaken or when special rules dictate otherwise (port rules often give right of way to big container vessels over all pleasure craft in restricted waters).
5. Sailcraft giving way should do so in good time and avoid crossing ahead of the right-of-way vessel.

This board rider must keep clear of the boat he is overtaking, but has right of way over the approaching centreboarder.

Safety

Like any water sport, sailboarding has potential dangers. But accidents are few and providing you are aware of the problems and take sensible care to avoid them, there is no reason why your sailboarding should not be happy and safe.

Know your limits

The major problems arise with inexperienced board sailors charging out into the unknown and suddenly finding they cannot get back. This is a very easy thing to do, particularly if the wind is offshore, for once you are up on the board and running before the wind, it all seems so easy and pleasant. Only when you turn round to head home do you find the wind has freshened, the chop has built up and the shore is a lot further away than you thought it was.

It is vitally important to know your limits and sail within them. Stay close to the beach until you are confident you can get back, even if weather conditions change. If you are experimenting or feeling adventurous, take a buddy with you. Two heads are always better than one, especially if one is experienced. And if you do sail alone or venture far out, always check the weather forecast beforehand and be prepared for any eventuality.

Check the gear

Nothing is more likely to cause problems when you are well out from the shore than gear failure. Make a thorough check of your gear before you set out, for there are no repair shops out at sea and even a tiny broken fitting can leave you stranded out on the horizon.

Wear the right clothes

As mentioned earlier, wetsuits are the only really satisfactory clothes for sailboarding unless you are just taking short hops off the beach. Life-jackets are important, also, and some of the better life-jackets have a harness attached, and back-pack pockets to carry basic requirements on long-haul sailing trips.

Check the weather

The wind is the most important part of the weather to a board sailor. A pleasant afternoon sea breeze which suddenly swings 180 degrees and turns into a roaring offshore blow can spell disaster. If the wind is onshore, no matter how strong, you can, at worst, drift back. But watch those changes that result in winds blowing out to sea.

Emergency

Despite all the careful precautions, an emergency can arise when sailboarding. And when it happens, it happens quickly. Two basic requirements must be observed no matter what the emergency, and these are: STAY WITH THE BOARD and AVOID PANIC.

The latter is directly related to the first—if you stay with the board, which will provide a totally adequate survival platform the whole time, there is no danger, and therefore no need to panic.

Panicking and making a swim for it can spell disaster. Even if the shore looks invitingly close, it is farther away than you think. Cramp or unexpected currents could get you long before you reach it. And hypothermia is always lurking around in cold water. Think of it this way: It is always easier and safer to paddle the board than swim.

Distress signals

It is not possible nor practical for sailboards to be fitted with flares or other recognised distress signals. If you are in trouble, stand on the board and wave your arms over your head. Everyone knows this to be a call for help and it should soon bring assistance.

Self-rescue

Broken gear, bad weather or lack of wind can cause you to be stranded offshore and out of sight of rescuers. When this happens, the following procedure will get you home safely:
1. Pull out the mast foot from the step.
2. Release the outhaul, and fold the mast and boom together.
3. Roll up the sail and secure everything together with outhaul and uphaul lines, using half hitches.
4. Stow all the gear on the board, kneel or lie down and start to paddle. Note: It is easier to paddle a board across wind and waves in a diagonal line than punch directly into them.

Emergency stopping

One of the great things about sailboards is that you can stop them very easily when trouble arises. The simplest and most effective way to stop in an emergency is to drop the rig in the water.

The board will lurch to a halt in a matter of a metre or so, when you can gather your thoughts, assess the situation and start all over again.

There are other more spectacular ways of stopping the board such as the stop gybe, but these require a considerable amount of skill and are for the experts only.

Hypothermia

At temperatures below 20 degrees C the body cannot regenerate heat as quickly as it is lost. Prolonged exposure to such temperatures therefore means a constant loss of body heat. Initially this affects only the surface and sub-surface areas of the body as the blood supply to outer extremities is reduced to protect the temperature of vital organs. But if the exposure is continued, the cold penetrates to deep body areas and vital organs cease to function.

Board sailors, even in relatively warm climates, risk hypothermia if they do not wear the correct clothing to prevent heat loss. For prolonged sailing, a neoprene wetsuit is the only sure protection. These suits come in different forms so that the right amount of protection is provided for the existing conditions. The nearest substitute, but one which can be used only for limited periods of exposure, is a tight-fitting woolly jumper worn directly against the skin.

For extended sailing or in cool conditions, a full wetsuit with jacket and full leg pants is essential to ward off hypothermia.

Symptoms

The tell-tale symptoms of approaching hypothermia are:
- Severe, often uncontrollable shivering.
- Fingers and toes lose sensation, lips turn blue.
- Feelings of weakness and anxiety.
- Lack of co-ordination and slurred speech.

Self-treatment

If you feel the symptoms of hypothermia coming on, your immediate actions can mean the difference between safety and hospitalisation.
- Do not leave the board.
- Stay out of the water.
- Do not attempt to sail.
- Prevent further heat loss by curling up in the foetal position and wrapping the sail around you.

Further treatment

The key to successful recovery from hypothermia is to re-heat the body **slowly**. Fast reheating can be as lethal as the cold. Hot baths and similar severe treatment are definitely out. Blankets, warm, dry clothing, the heat of another body wrapped in with the victim — all are sensible ways of restoring the body heat slowly so that the colder blood of the extremities is gradually warmed, and not driven farther into the body core.

Well designed board wetsuits create comfort and safety in all conditions. Jackets can be removed, pants unzipped and bib rolled down to the waist in very warm conditions.

Strong wind sailing

Sailing a board in winds over 10 to 15 knots requires special techniques. Unlike a sailboat which can relieve pressure in the sail solely by easing the sheet, a sailboard needs other ways to reduce the strain or it will become very unbalanced. The best method is to pull the mast to windward over the board which effectively reduces the sail surface presented to the wind and thus reduce the pressure in the sail. There are other methods and, of course, a smaller sail can also be used. If the wind is consistently strong, then changing down to a smaller sail becomes necessary, but often the pressure needs to be relieved only temporarily in a gust, and the full sail area maintained at other times. In this case, reducing the pressure by heeling the mast to windward will usually suffice.

The procedure for getting under way in strong winds is as follows:

1. Adopt the usual starting position as described earlier.
2. Pull the sail up fairly quickly, for if it fills with wind while the clew is into the water it will pull out of your hands.
3. Tilt the mast forward and at the same time pull it over the board to windward.
4. Lean backwards, taking the mast with you, and sheet on at the same time with your back hand. This must be well co-ordinated for if you sheet on too quickly, you will be pulled forward into the water, and if you do not sheet on fast enough you will fall backwards into the water!

45

5. Set your front foot just ahead of the mast, and brace your back foot well back along the board. The stronger the wind, the farther back over the water you must lean.

Closing up

Closing up comes easily when sailing in strong winds for the board responds quickly to even the slightest backwards tilt of the mast. The important part of this manoeuvre is to prevent her racing up into the wind and stalling, for like a frisky horse, once she gets the bit between her teeth she will want to do her own thing!

Bearing away

Bearing away from the wind is more difficult, for tilting the mast forward means exposing more sail area to the wind, pulling you forward off balance. Once again the secret lies with pulling the mast to windward and leaning hard back. Controlling the pressure with the sheet hand can help relieve the weight of the rig, but this is a manoeuvre which takes some getting used to in strong wind conditions.

Planing

When the board gets up speed she will be skipping across the surface with only the dagger board effectively in the water. If the board heels to one side or the other, the dagger board will act as a hydroplane and flip the board over. This is usually preceded by severe swinging from side to side and the solution lies in lifting the dagger board half way. Not an easy thing to do when the board is flying along at speed and somewhat unstable to boot. The best approach is to close up to the wind and let the sail flap while you reach down and pull up the dagger board.

Luffing

The sail operates most effectively when it is full and drawing hard. In strong winds this may be too much to hold, and even with the mast set well to windward, the pressure in the sail may be too great. The correct solution would be to change down to a smaller sail, but if the strong gusts are only of short duration, as is the case in normal sailing, the pressure can be eased by easing the back hand and letting the sail luff.

Luffing is the term given to slight collapse of the sail along its leading edge (luff). It is not acceptable for good sailing except in the conditions described above where temporary relief of pressure in the sail is essential. Experienced board sailors can also use the luff when sailing hard on the wind by nosing the board just within the non-sailing zone for the moment of the gust, then pulling her back again. This is definitely not recommended for any but the very experienced, since it requires a high degree of skill, and even the sightest misjudgement may mean disaster.

Racing

Racing is beneficial to sailboarders of all standards. Beginners can benefit by just hanging around near (not on!) the course and watching how the experts do it. Intermediates can get into the thrills of racing, gradually building up their skills and expertise by competing against better sailors. And the experts themselves can enjoy the superb thrill of competition at the same time adding polish to their skills.

Racing is controlled by the International Yacht Racing Union which lays down a set of rules that cover racing in any part of the world. The IYRU also lays down specifications for racing courses, and the most common of these is known as the 'Olympic' course, since it is widely used at the Olympic Games.

The course consists of three basic legs in the form of a triangle, one leg of which is directly to windward. Since sailing to windward is the greatest test of any sailor's skill, the windward leg is often sailed three times. The basic course is widely used for all sailcraft races, from sailboards to International 12 metres.

The racing rules

Racing any sail craft involves using the rule book to its fullest extent. Tactics are very much a part of racing, and tactics revolve around using the rules to gain advantage over other competitors at all points in the race. Obviously, all board sailors involved in racing should be thoroughly familiar with the rule book and able to put it into practice during a race.

Speed

The very word 'racing' means speed, and this is the basic essential of all racing manoeuvres. The board must be kept moving at her top pace throughout the entire length of the race. This involves perfect sail setting, maximum drive and fast manoeuvring, particularly on the windward leg and around the marks where competitors will be using every tactic in the book to disadvantage you and slow your board.

Clear wind

Without clear wind, the board will not be moving at her best. Competitors will consistently try to disadvantage your board by fouling your wind. This is particularly the case at the start, when all boards in the race will be concentrated into one small area. The windward position is always the most advantageous position since any board downwind will not obtain clear, undisturbed air.

Starboard tack

If you have a starboard tack, then every sailboard on a port tack must give way to you. And since giving way means either tacking or going behind you, the advantage to be gained is obvious.

Reading the wind

This has nothing to do with the rule book, but greatly influences the outcome of a race. As a rule, sailboards are very much influenced by windshifts. Local knowledge of the surrounding terrain, a basic grounding on the technical aspects of wind behaviour and a sharp eye for the signs of wind shifts will pay handsome dividends in a race.

Using a harness

The harness is used to take the weight of the rig off your arms and transfer it to your body. Although some harnesses are incorporated in life-jackets, all are designed so that the full weight of the rig is spread across shoulders and waist, without losing any control. Fitting and using a harness is as follows:
1. Attach the harness lines to the boom. The lines should be at least a metre long and hang down about 15 cm (6 in.) from the boom.
2. Hook on the harness. There is no specific method, but most people have the hook facing down.
3. Put a little body weight on the harness and slide the hook along the line until the rig feels balanced. Use your back hand to trim the sail.
4. Lean out and take the weight with your shoulders, bend your knees, not your hips. You will soon get the feel of your body taking the weight of the rig, leaving your arms to control the boom.

Footwork

The more familiar you become with your board, the more you will appreciate how valuable your feet can be in controlling the board's movements. While most of the control so far has been related to the sail, footwork on the board can not only relieve a lot of the sail work, but can compliment it by providing dual control and therefore faster response.

Turning the board, for example, particularly on a reach or run, can be speeded up enormously by pushing down with one foot on the opposite side (termed the 'rail'). When close-hauled, the board can be made to round up into the wind by pushing away with the back foot, or to bear away from the wind by pushing away with the front foot. With practice, such footwork can increase the board's manoeuvrability enormously, and such exercises quickly take you from the novice stage into advanced class.

Like changing gears in a car, footwork and handwork must be co-ordinated into a smooth, easy action if the best performance is to be achieved. This only comes with practice and experience, and watching how the experts do it.

Freestyle

This is the term given to the spectacular 'trick' sailing done by those who can really sail their board. It is a kind of gymnastics on a sailboard and calls for high degrees of skill. It has many advantages other than the sheer satisfaction of good performance. It is a first class exercise, it teaches experts newer and more sophisticated tricks and it teaches non-experts how to gain higher skills. Most of all it teaches total control of the board.

The water start

There are a number of tricks that are standard freestyle practices, but the limit to new techniques is purely the limit of your imagination and skill. Many freestyle actions are not tricks at all, but useful sailing techniques. Just such a technique is the water-start, which, as its name denotes, enables the board to be started and sailed from the in-water position. The procedure requires winds of around 15 knots and above to provide sufficient weight to lift your body out of the water.

1. Get the mast over to the windward side of the board and raise it a little to allow the wind to get beneath it.
2. Get your legs onto the board, one on either side of the mast. You may need to grasp the mast and sail low down to achieve this.
3. Swing the board into the wind a little and raise the mast until the wind gets well under it. As soon as the sail fills and pulls you into the upright position, get into the correct sailing position and start sailing normally.

Sailing clew first

This is an exercise in sail handing techniques. It involves sailing the board with the sail reversed — that is, the clew or end of the boom pointing forward. The procedure is as follows:

1. While sailing in the normal position, grasp the mast low down with the front hand and release the back hand.
2. As the boom swings away, change hands.
3. When the boom has swung 180 degrees, grab it with the front hand and take up the normal stance and grip. The board will begin to sail with the sail reversed.

Railriding

The most common of the more advanced freestyle techniques, railriding involves sailing the board on its edge. The procedure is relatively simple, but like all freestyle techniques, requires a great deal of practice:

1. Sail normally on a reach in winds around 10 to 15 knots.
2. Press down on the lee rail (side) with your back foot, holding the boom for support.
3. Squat down and put your front foot under the windward rail and flip the board up onto its edge.
4. Transfer your weight onto the shins of your forward leg as you lever yourself to the upright position with both feet on the top rail of the board.
5. Balancing carefully on the top rail, sail the board in the normal manner.

Back-to-back — another form of freestyle.

Wave riding

The ultimate thrill and exhilaration for sailboarders comes with sailing in big waves. In no other sport is the challenge of the elements so complete, for wave sailing is a combination of both sailing and surfing and requires a high degree of skill in both. Wave jumping is the greatest test of wave sailing and is a further extension of the skills of both sailing and surfing. It goes without saying that novice board sailors should not attempt even modest wave sailing until they are totally competent at sailing in still waters.

A good way to get the feel of wave riding in quieter waters is to ride the wash of passing boats, particularly large vessels. Some estuaries have modest waves, particularly near their exit to the ocean. By practicing on these smaller waves, the feel of riding a 'bucking' board will soon be mastered and it is then time to take the board to the ocean beach.

Once again, practice on the smaller waves. Surf waves break only in the vicinity of the beach, so initially paddle your board out beyond the break and start sailing the rollers where they are just big undulations. It will take a lot of practice in these rollers before you are ready to challenge the big white 'walls' near the beach.

Hints on wave riding

It is not possible in a booklet such as this to provide detail of the highly skilled sport of wave riding. However, a few hints and tips will not go astray:
- Be very careful your skeg does not touch bottom in the shallow water near the beach or it will snap off.
- Take care not to spill in the steep waves close to the beach. This is where the rig is most likely to be damaged.
- Always keep the board moving fast when among the waves. Only in this way can it be kept under total control.
- Pick the right spot on the wave to make your approach—a low, shallow face for preference. Try to jump the wave before it breaks.
- As you approach the face, sheet in hard and push down with your back foot to lift the bow of the board up over the crest.
- If you become airborne, let off the sail so it luffs immediately. On landing, tilt the mast forward and sheet on again.

Surfing

Riding in on a breaking wave requires high skills but is the most rewarding aspect of wave riding. Once again, there is only room here for a few hints and tips:

- Watch your waves. Note how a surfer picks the right wave before making his run. The right wave makes all the difference to the way the board rides. It must not be too close to breaking when you start your run.
- At first, head shorewards down the face until you have enough speed to outrun the wave.
- Steer upwind a little to traverse the face and watch for the start of the break.
- Bear away as the wave begins to break.
- Stay just in front of the breaking wave as it surges into the beach.
- When the wave has crumbled and the beach is close, sheet in and head across the white water to avoid a spill and risk damaging the rig.
- Since body weight and foot control are vital in wave riding of any kind, you should use a board with foot straps in preference to a standard sailboard.

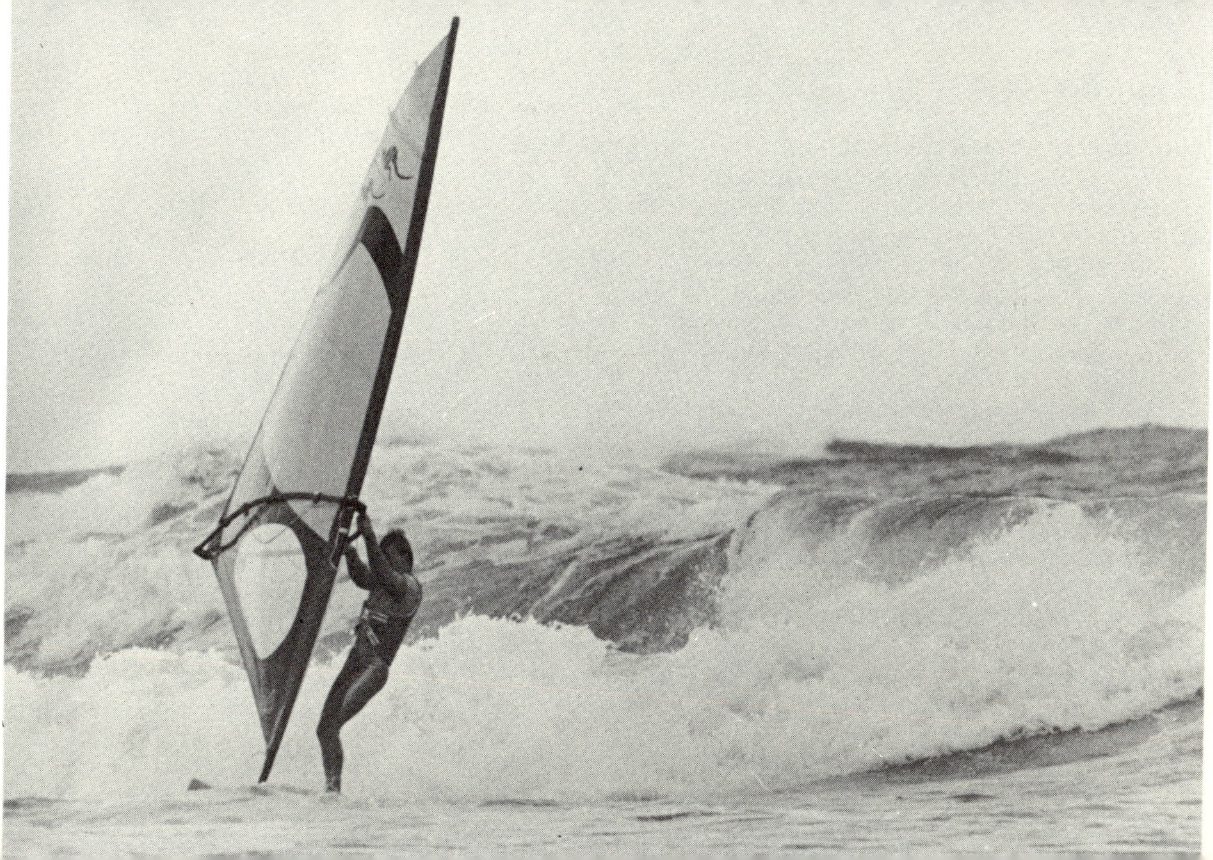

Etiquette

Much of etiquette concerns commonsense and courtesy. Other people enjoy the water, although not necessarily on a sailboard. While the beaches and waterways are getting more crowded by the day, there is plenty of room for everyone. Consideration for others is a basic maxim of any sport and is the hallmark of a true sportsman. A few points worth bearing in mind when sailboarding:

1. If you are practising and likely to fall, get well away from the beach, especially well away from swimmers and young children.
2. Although it may impress the more immature spectators, screaming into the beach at speed can cause serious injury to youngsters at the water's edge.
3. When you must give way to another craft, do so in plenty of time. Playing 'chicken' with a flying sailboard is only practiced by immature riders.
4. Don't push your right of way to the limit. Remember it is far easier for a sailboard to manoeuvre than a 20-metre yacht.
5. Until you are very experienced, do not sail in channels used by ocean-going ships and other commercial craft. Apart from the danger, it may be against local maritime laws.

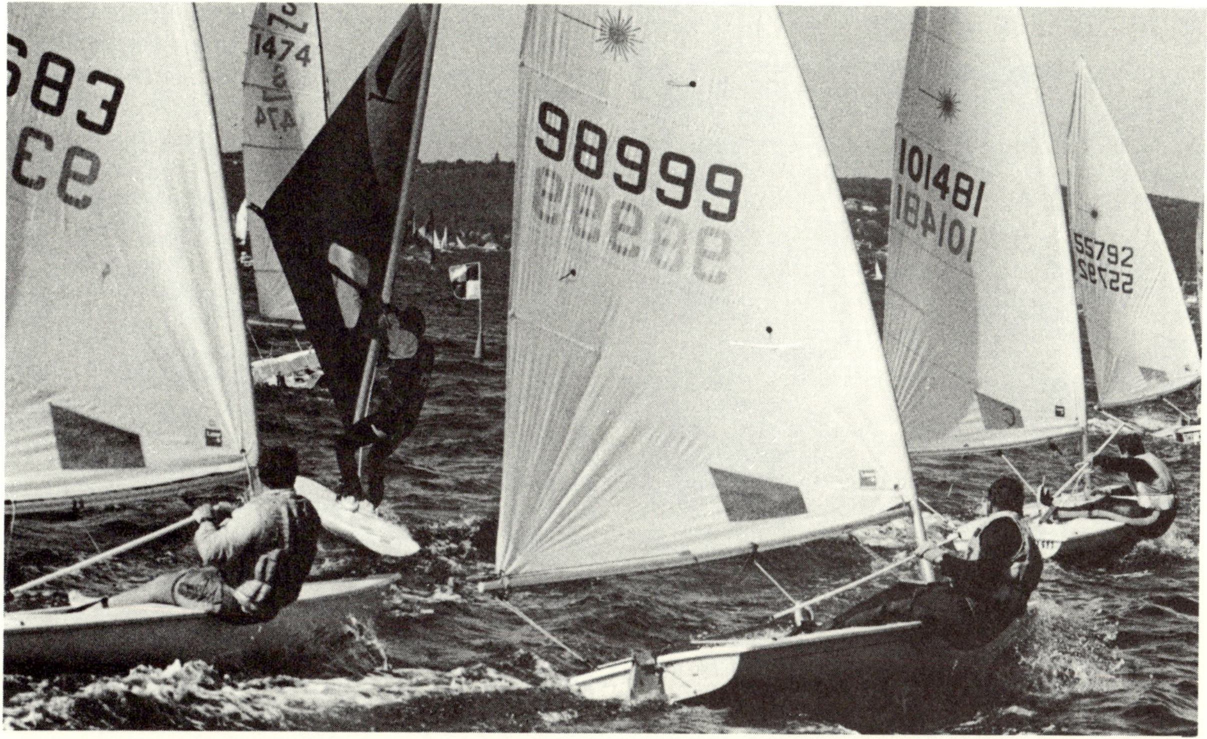
683
1474
98999
101481
55792

Four popular sailboarding knots

Clove hitch. *Often used for securing the inhaul to the mast. Pass the end around the mast and cross it over itself. Pass it round the mast again but this time cross it under itself.*

Figure-of-eight knot. *A useful knot for preventing a rope running through an eye or cleat. Hold the end of the rope in your right hand and the standing part in the left. Place the end over the standing part, under it, and back over itself to pass through the loop thus created from the top to the bottom.*

Prusik hitch. *Common hitch for securing the inhaul to the mast. Form an eye in the rope with one end longer than the other. Pass the two free ends round the mast and through the eye. Repeat the procedure, bringing the two ends up through the eye the second time between the previous turns, as illustrated.*

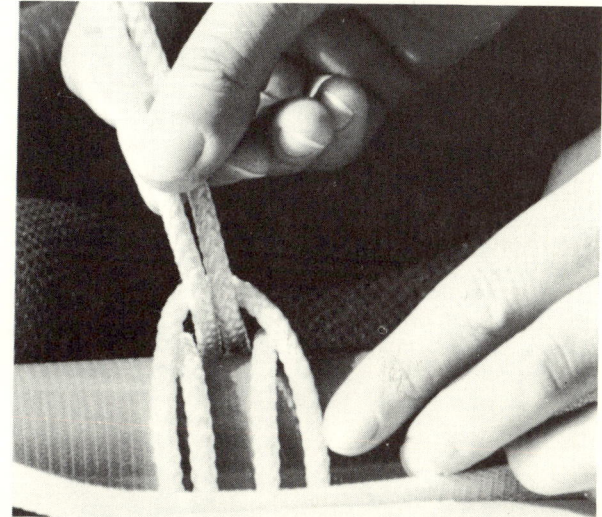

Two half hitches. *Used for securing the downhaul. Pass the end of the rope through the eye, the back over itself, around and under its own standing part. Repeat to form a second half hitch.*

Some popular sailing terms

Abeam	At right angles to the line of the board
Aft	Behind. Towards the back
Astern	Behind
Back to back	Freestyle sailing technique
Barging	Illegal tactic at start of a race
Batten	Stiffener placed in leech of sail
Beam	Same as abeam. Also the width of the board
Beam reach	Reaching with wind abeam
Bear away	Turn away from the wind
Beating	Another term for tacking to windward
Boom	The spar that stretches the sail from the mast
Bow	Front tip of the board
Bowline	Non-slip loop tied in a rope
Broad reach	Reaching with the wind behind the beam
CLR	Centre of Lateral Resistance
C of E or CE	Centre of Effort
Cleat	Securing point for rope end
Clew	Aft corner of the sail
Close-hauled	Sailing as close to the wind as possible
Close reach	Reaching with the wind ahead of the beam
Close up	Turn towards the wind
Clove hitch	Useful knot
Course	The track along which the board sails
Dagger board	The fin projecting beneath the board
Downhaul	The rope that tensions the sail downwards
Figure-of-eight	A type of stopper knot
Fibreglass	Resin and glass fibre composite
Foot	Bottom edge of sail
Footstraps	Board fittings in which feet are placed
Forward	Ahead
Freestyle	Expert techniques in sailboarding

Gybe	Tacking with the wind behind	Mark	Turning buoy on race course
Handle	Front point of the boom	Mast	Spar on which sail is mounted
Harness	Used to transer weight of rig from arms to body	Mast foot	Bottom of mast which plugs into board
Head dip	Leaning back until head touches the water	Mast step	Recess in board to take mast foot
Head to wind	Board pointing directly into the wind	Off the wind	Sailing anywhere but close to the wind
Hotdogging	Another term for some freestyle techniques	Offshore	Away from the shoreline
Hypothermia	Medical condition resulting from exposure	Olympic course	Special racing course with one leg into the wind
Inhaul	Line use to secure mast to boom	On the wind	Sailing close to the wind
IYRU	International Yacht Racing Union	Outhaul	Line that secures clew of sail to the boom
Leash	Line securing mast foot to board	Peak	Top corner of sail
Leech	Back or trailing edge of sail	Polyethylene	Plastic material used to make boards
Leeward	Opposite to the direction of the wind	Port	Left side facing forward
Luff	Front or leading edge of sail	Port tack	Sailing with wind coming over port side
Luffing	Sail collapsing along front edge	Prusik hitch	Knot used for securing inhaul to mast
		Pumping	Working the boom back and forth to fill sail
		Railriding	Freestyle technique

Reaching	Sailing with wind abeam
Running free	Sailing with wind right astern
Sheeting	Pulling the boom in or letting it out
Skeg	Tiny fin under back of board
Starboard	Right hand side facing forward
Starboard tack	Sailing with wind on starboard side
Start position	Back to wind, feet on either side of mast step
Stern	After end of board
Surfing	Riding in with breaking waves
Swell	Large, non-breaking waves
Tack	Front corner of sail.
Tacking	Changing from one tack to another
Tactics	Using racing rules to gain advantage in race
Trough	Hollow between waves
True wind	Direction of wind away from moving board
Universal joint	Fitting at foot of mast
Uphaul	Rope used to lift rig from water
Upwind	In the direction of the wind
Water start	Sailing from the in-water position
Wave jumping	Sailing out over the crests of big surf
Wave sailing	Sailing in surf or big waves
Weather	The side the wind is coming from
White water	Shoreward side of breaking surf
Window	Plastic see-through section of sail
Wind shifts	Changes in wind direction
Windsurfer	Brand name for popular sailboard
Windward	On the side the wind is coming from